The Miracle of Greg

Betsy M. Haas

Dedication

This book is dedicated to the memory of Greg and to all the homeless kitties that are scared and alone, waiting for their chance to be safe and free, to play and relax, to go on nice adventures, and to share love with new family and friends. May we all get to experience the loving relationship between pets and people.

About the Author

Betsy Haas was born in her mother's family home in the small historic railroad town of Whistler, Alabama. She attended Huntingdon College in Montgomery and later continued her studies at the University of South Alabama. She studied art under several local teachers and in various workshops in the Mobile/Fairhope, Alabama area and had her paintings on display in local galleries. Betsy put aside her artwork to help found and develop the Animal Rescue Foundation, which became one of Mobile's largest and most effective nonprofit dog and cat rescue groups. In 2007, Betsy founded Aide for Animals (www.aideforanimals.org), another nonprofit animal welfare organization which has been very active operating as a sanctuary and adoption center for unwanted, disabled and special needs animals in her community. Betsy has always put the welfare of others before her own, whether it is for animals or people.

Once, there was a darling little orphaned kitten named Greg who, after being lost in the woods for most of his young life, was found and happily adopted by Grandpa Tom and Grandma Betsy, a couple who loved animals and had already adopted quite a few.

One cold Friday morning, just a few days before Christmas and after Grandma Betsy had carefully prepared breakfast for their dog, Miss Lillie, and their hungry kittens, it was time for the special task of putting up the final holiday decorations.

There was a Christmas tree next to the big fireplace in the kitchen trimmed with shiny lights, all kinds of wonderful ornaments, and, at the very top, a beautiful, silvery star that actually twinkled.

Greg seemed quite fascinated with that tree! Sure, it must have been much fancier than any of the other ones he had seen, but it still had the sweet smell of the woods he would remember.

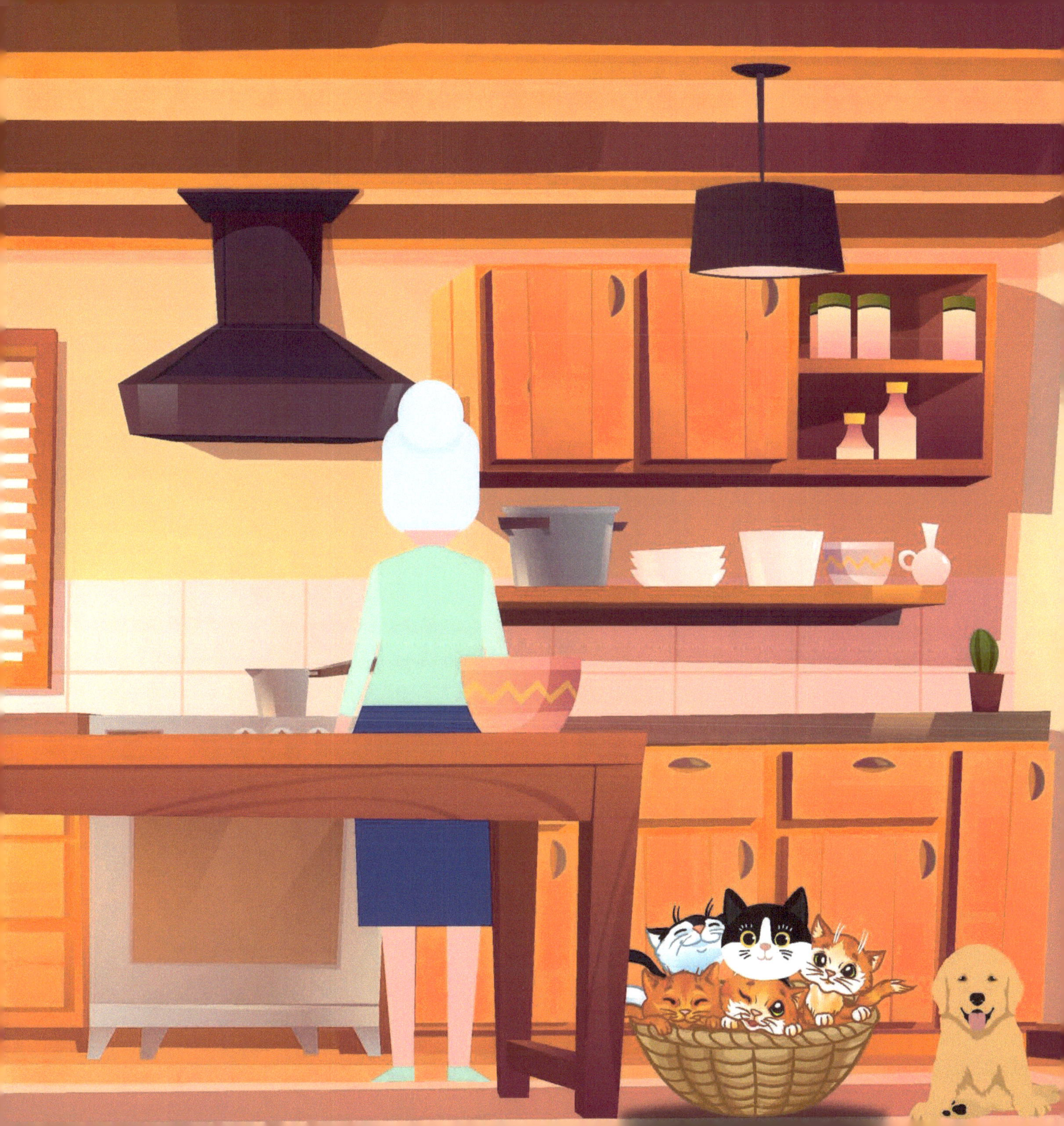

Grandma had put pine garlands and sprigs of Holly here and there, and a big wreath with a red bow on it over the mantle. She so wanted their home to look its best for the holidays. And filling the whole house with such smells as bayberry, pine, cinnamon, apple pie, and gingerbread was one of her favorite things to do.

Sometimes, Greg would sit under the tree with his little nose turned upward and his eyes squeezed shut, sniffing the fragrant air.

Each morning after breakfast, the other kittens would go outside to play. Greg would stay inside and amuse himself by chasing imaginary playmates. Jumping and diving, he would get his back all humped up and do his "crab walk," grabbing and twisting back and forth and walking sideways. He looked so happy! It was a good life for a once-homeless little fellow.

He got special attention too, since he was the newest and youngest. When Grandma would pick him up and nuzzle him under her chin, he would purr.

But, that morning, he looked outside through the frosty windows and saw Grandpa raking leaves. The other kittens were romping and running after leaves and playing tag, and there was a brown squirrel watching from a perch on an overhead limb.

Everyone looked like they were having so much fun! Greg ran back and forth from the door to Grandma, mewing and mewing, standing on his hind legs and looking up at her with such a wistful look that she gave in. With a loving pat on the head, she put him out on the porch to play with the other kittens, telling him to be a good boy and stay near the house.

That afternoon, after Grandma had finished her housework and decorating the house, she left for the market to do the grocery shopping, picking out all their favorite foods and planning the evening meal. Then, she went on to the pet store to pick up special treats of catnip for her darlings and a nice, tasty bone for sweet Miss Lillie.

As she drove back into the yard, the precious kittens ran to meet her; Miss Lillie wagged her tail and gave out a few short barks as her greeting. They were all so happy Grandma was home, and they were ready for their supper! Grandma carefully made sure each and every animal had plenty to eat while Grandpa gave them lots of fresh, clean water. She then gave them all a big hug, and with full tummies, they all cuddled up in their basket as contented as could be.

After supper, Grandma and Grandpa sank into their favorite chairs. What a busy day it had been!

Some of the kittens climbed on her lap, purring and kneading, making their "kitty biscuits," while Miss Lillie and some of the others shared a chair with Grandpa Tom.

PET SHOP

Then, all of a sudden, Grandma sat up with a start! She realized she hadn't seen Greg since that morning, and here it was nighttime! How could she have overlooked him?!

She and Grandpa quickly put the kittens in their basket, hurried outside, and called and pleaded for him to come in for his supper while they looked everywhere.

At midnight, they were still calling, but Greg was nowhere to be seen. They were heartbroken. It was cold outside, and the next night, there was to be a hard freeze.

As they gave up the search for the night, big tears rolled down Grandma's cheeks, and Grandpa shook his head in sadness.

She and Grandpa Tom hardly slept that night wondering where in the world Greg could be. Bright and early the next morning, as soon as everyone had their breakfast, Grandma started calling her friends. So far, no one had seen the little kitten. Now, she was really getting frantic. There was still no Greg, and it would freeze that night.

Grandma Betsy finally reached one of her neighbors, Jack, who told her a kitten had been at his house the day before, playing in the back of his nephew's truck. His nephew had gone home, but maybe had seen the kitten. Jack would be happy to call him and would let her know.

It was beginning to get dark. She was sick with worry; all she could think about was the freeze that night and little Greg being alone and cold.

It was time to feed the others their supper. Grandma and Grandpa tried their best to look happy for their darlings but had to fight back tears of sadness over Greg's absence.

Now it was late, and there was no word from their neighbor. Grandma cried and cried, and she and Grandpa had another sleepless night.

The next morning, after feeding the others and assuring all of them how much they were loved, Grandma Betsy called her neighbor. Jack had spoken with his nephew, and yes, he had seen the kitten on his truck. Greg must have been in it when the nephew left for a job over eighteen miles away!

 She got the address where the nephew had gone the day before; her hopes were up! She couldn't wait another minute. Greg had been gone since Friday, and here it was Sunday! She had to find Greg and bring him home!

Those eighteen miles seemed to take forever! In the car on the way over, Grandma Betsy prayed. "God, I know I ask you for too many favors, but please, just one more."

After knocking on doors and talking with the people in the neighborhood, about thirty minutes later, three little girls excitedly told her they had seen a nice lady take a little kitten off a truck and put him in her house! It had to be Greg! Grandma's prayer was answered. She just knew he was safe!

Grandma ran to the lady's house. As she rang the doorbell, she and Greg saw each other through the glass. When the lady opened the door, he ran and jumped into Grandma's arms, purring so loudly he could probably be heard down the block! The lady was so happy for them. She had seen the scared, cold little kitten on the truck Friday afternoon and knew he was in danger. So, she had put him inside where he would be safe and warm.

After thanking the nice lady over and over, Grandma got back in her car with Greg in her arms. She sat there hugging him and crying tears of joy. They were going home!

When they arrived back home, Grandpa Tom's mouth flew open. Hardly able to believe his eyes, he and the others ran out to meet them. Grandpa and Grandma stood there hugging Greg for a long time while all the other kittens and Miss Lillie looked up with great big smiles on their faces.

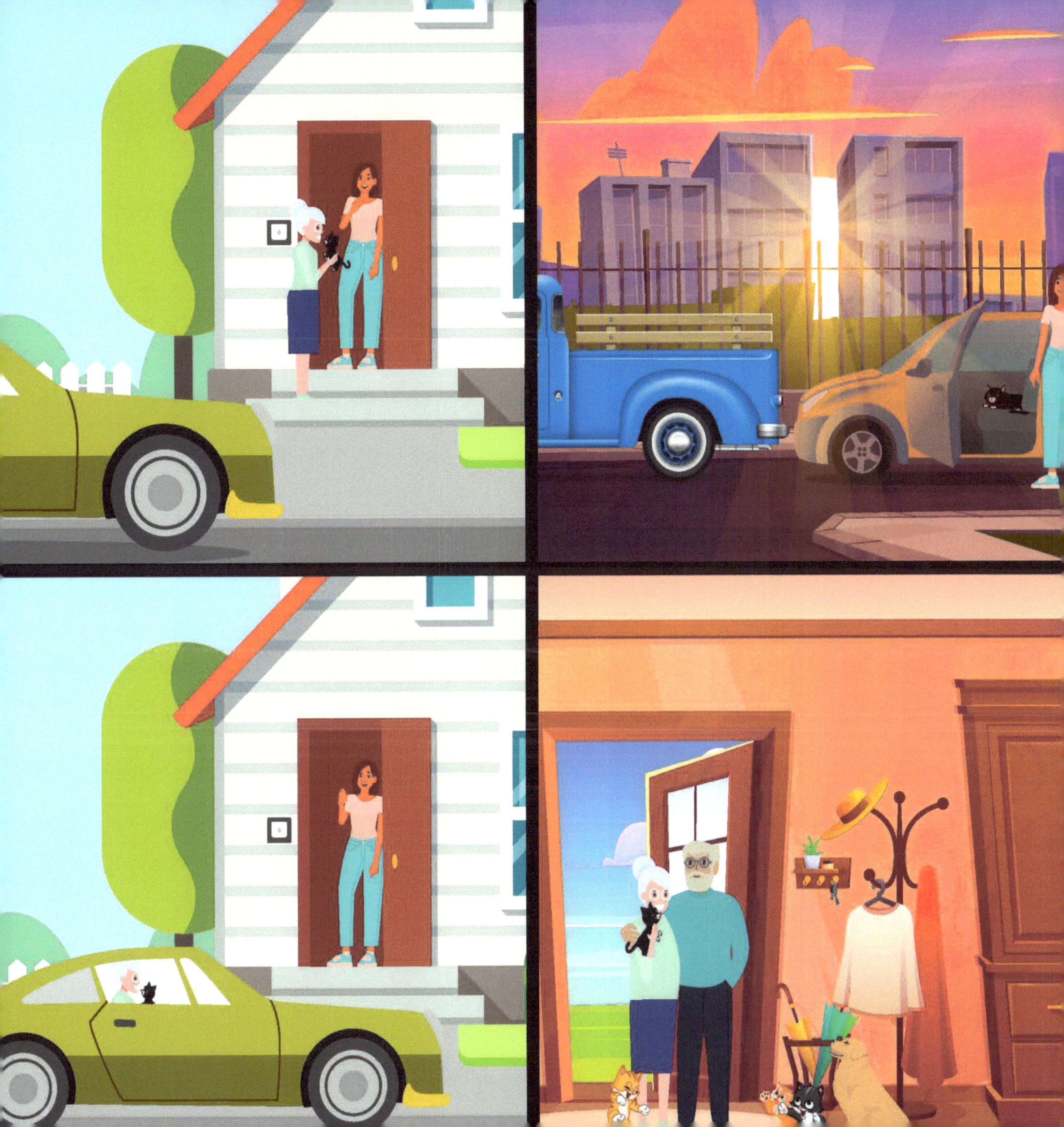

They took Greg, Miss Lillie, and all the other kittens into the kitchen where Grandpa
had made a nice, cozy fire.

Grandma poured them all a bowl of warm milk and a bowl for Miss Lillie too. This was
a very special occasion! Finding Greg and having him home again was truly a miracle!

Then, the room lit up! They all looked up at the Christmas tree. The star on top was
shining brighter than ever as if to say, "Welcome home, Greg!"

What a wonderful day it had turned out to be, and Christmas was going to be even
better!

THE END